D1240796

KAWAII
Tarot

KAWAII
Tarot

UNDERSTANDING
TAROT WITH THE
KAWAII UNIVERSE

ILLUSTRATIONS BY
Lulu Mayo

ROCK
POINT

CONTENTS

INTRODUCTION

Welcome to the wonderful world of kawaii! In this book, we will explore the practice of tarot through the eyes of super-cute and cuddly kawaii creatures. Kawaii is a Japanese term that roughly translates to "cute" in English, though "kawaii" is more of a concept. It can be used to describe people, clothes, characters and even handwriting. If you're a fan of Hello Kitty or Pusheen the Cat, then you know the kawaii universe.

If you're already a lover of all things kawaii or you're simply a fan in general of the uber-colorful and adorable, then you're in the right place! Using kawaii creatures to explain the art of tarot is a creative way to foster the connection between the reader and the cards. This connection is crucial in practicing tarot; without that, it can be like two people speaking different languages: You might have an idea of what the cards are trying to communicate, but it will be difficult for the cards to speak to you in a meaningful way.

There are nearly as many different ways to design tarot cards as there are people. Just about every kind of thing that people are interested in has its own tarot deck. Do you like cats, goth music, trees, Salvador Dali, feminism, Jungian archetypes, rainbows, or the sitcom The Golden Girls? Then there is a tarot deck out there for you.

When you are ready, you can explore the different types of decks that are available to you and choose the one that speaks to you the most. As long as you find a deck with 78 cards, then you can take what you learn in these pages and apply them to your own personal tarot practice to learn to use your intuition to interpret the cards' messages and connect with your inner guidance system to help you determine your next move

BEGINNER'S GUIDE TO THE TAROT

What the tarot is: A FRIENDLY, WISE, MYSTERIOUS, AND SOMETIMES FRUSTRATING GUIDE TO THE PATHS THAT YOUR LIFE HAS ALREADY TAKEN AND COULD TAKE IN THE FUTURE.

What the tarot is not: A HYPER-SPECIFIC, FOR-CERTAIN, CHOOSE YOUR OWN ADVENTURE ANSWER KEY THAT CAN PREDICT WITH ABSOLUTE CERTAINTY EVERYTHING THAT COULD POTENTIALLY HAPPEN TO YOU. EVER.

A (Very) Little History

The practice of tarot and tarot cards have been around for centuries in various forms. Some researchers have detected symbols and themes that can potentially be traced as far back as ancient Egypt. Most histories date them to the early fifteenth century in Italy, to a card game known as tarocchi that was popular with the nobility.

Around three hundred years later, the game of tarot began to be seen in a more spiritual and magical aspect in France and later in England. In the nineteenth century, it became popular to use tarot cards for seeking knowledge about or understanding of the future. The basic format of tarot that we know today was also created at this time: a 78-card deck designed with symbols meant to represent either stages of or influences on your life.

TAKE CARE OF YOUR CARDS AND THEY WILL TAKE CARE OF YOU

What tarot novices may not realize is the importance of caring for your cards. Don't start out thinking that the cards are just a way to get answers. If reading tarot was that simple, then there would not be much to learn. In that case, each card would have one single fixed meaning for everyone in all situations. This would make for much quicker but also very boring and unenlightening readings.

Think of your tarot deck not as a utilitarian object but something that you are connected with in a special and unique way. These cards might have come out of a box and look like many others of its kind, but once they are in your hands and in your home, you are bonded. That means you should take care of them—because vibes matter. It's true!

First, you should cleanse them. Also called attuning, this is basically a process that removes all the spiritual yuck that might have accumulated on the cards in transit to your home. There are several ways to do this:

- Burn a smudge stick or even just some incense that you like in the room where you will be keeping the cards. If you want to, hold the cards in the smoke. If you would rather your cards do not smell like smoke, then don't do this. Do whatever feels right for you!
- Leave them out overnight in a spot where they will be doused in the light of the full moon.
- Holding the deck in your hand, think positive, happy thoughts. Visualize those ideas running into the cards themselves.
- Put them in order and then shuffle again.

Now, make sure that you have a good place to store the cards. Some people insist on boxes carved with mystical runes and speckled with protective spells. Other people like to sleep near their cards, so they put them in their nightstand drawer or under their pillow. A simpler but still caring method is to wrap them in a cloth, possibly the one you use to lay them on when reading, and store them where they will be close to you. Natural materials (wood, cloth, silk) are preferable to unnatural (plastic). But again, what matters most is that you are caring and respectful towards your cards. After all, you are going to be asking them some important questions.

Question to ask your tarot: I FEEL STUCK. WHAT CAN I DO TO START A NEW PATH IN LIFE?

Question not to ask your tarot: MONEY WOULD BE GREAT. AM I GOING TO WIN THE LOTTERY?

READING TAROT
∽ GETTING STARTED ∽

The best way to get started is to just practice with your tarot cards. Spend a week or two shuffling your deck and going trough the cards at random. Don't feel any need to think about what the designs mean. Clear your head. Let your thoughts run free. Think in general terms about what you would like to talk to the cards about. Once you feel comfortable with your cards, you can have a better chance of hearing what they are saying to you. Some people like to keep a notebook and write down impressions of the cards that they can refer to later.

Then prepare a good spot for conducting your readings. Remember what we said about vibes: Your environment should reflect you. You can play music but you should avoid clutter and distractions. The most important thing is that you are relaxed in the space and have enough room to lay out your cards. Where possible, try to use the same setting repeatedly. So think ahead of time whether you may be reading for other people and leave room for them. After you have had your cards for at least a week or two and are feeling attuned to them, then you are ready to have your first reading.

WHO IS WHO?

The Reader – THE PERSON SHUFFLING, LAYING DOWN, TURNING, AND INTERPRETING THE CARDS.

The Querent – THE PERSON FOR WHOM THE CARDS ARE BEING INTERPRETED.

Shuffle the deck. You can do this a few different ways:

☞ Cut the deck by separating the cards into different stacks and then rearranging their order.

☞ Riffle the cards. This is what they call it when you split the deck in half, hold each half in one hand with your thumb on the top card and slowly release each side so they interleave. This looks and sounds the coolest, but some people avoid it because it seems disrespectful to the cards.

☞ Spread the cards out face-down on your cloth or any clean surface (do not get the cards dirty). Mix them all up with both hands. Bring them back together and stack them into a deck.

Repeat all or any of these as often as you like until the cards feel ready. The method does not really matter. The important thing is to not do it absent-mindedly but to be fully in the moment and attentive to the cards fluttering through your hands.

Cut the deck into smaller, even piles. Stack them back together. When you feel the deck is ready, start selecting your card(s). These can either be pulled at random from the deck, off the top or bottom, or out of a jumble.

There are many different ways to lay out your tarot cards. You should choose the one that feels best for you (are you sensing a pattern?). Here are a few possibilities:

SINGLE CARD

The simplest spread and easiest for getting a quick answer for yourself or somebody else. Some people call this a daily reading because they use it for continual practice. Fan out or cut the deck, think of a question, and select a card.

THREE CARD

This is what most people do, especially when starting out. Draw three cards and lay them face-down, side by side. The left-hand card represents the past; the middle the present; and the right the future. You can mix this up in different ways (goal, obstacle, solution/seek, avoid, accept).

D I Y

As you may have guessed, reading tarot is not really about doing what everyone else does. It is about you and your cards. What matters is that you focus on yourself, the card or cards in front of you, and let the truth flow through you. As long as you are being truthful about what you feel and telling that truth to yourself or the person you are reading for, then that is what matters. You can even shuffle and re-draw the cards if you do not get a feeling for the first one.

TURNING CARDS

ONCE YOU HAVE YOUR CARDS SPREAD, TURN THEM OVER HORIZONTALLY, GOING LEFT TO RIGHT. IF YOU MAKE A MISTAKE AND GO VERTICAL SO THAT THE CARD IS UPSIDE DOWN, THIS IS CALLED A REVERSAL. IN THAT INSTANCE, TAKE WHAT YOU INITIALLY FEEL ABOUT THE CARD'S MEANING, OR WHAT WE SAY LATER HERE, AND TURN IT AROUND. YOU CAN EVEN DO THIS ON PURPOSE!

THE MAJOR ARCANA

If the tarot were a professional sport, these cards would be the big league. The 22 Major Arcana cards represent archetypes drawn from mythology and medieval society.

Given their status, and the fact that they are sometimes referred to as "trump" cards, these cards will more often concern deeper, more life-impacting matters. Although they can be read for their individual meanings, they can also be seen as part of a larger, even mythic journey.

Each card is numbered from one to 21, with The Fool as zero (which is kind of a step up, at one time that card was not even numbered). We will talk about the cards in numerical order, listing the most common attributes associated with them and some suggestions for how you can think through their implications.

Don't think of these descriptions as definitions or sure things. They are more like jumping-off points. The starting point of a journey into your inner self and your possible futures.

The world is full of risk. But wonders, too. Will you go searching? Will you take a chance? Are you comfortable with things not making sense? What are you willing to risk? Step on out. The world is waiting. But remember! This is a wild card.

The MAGICIAN

Look up. Now look down. Ground yourself but keep an eye on what is coming. Is it time to open yourself to possibilities? Do you have untapped potential? Something previously hidden could be coming to light.

15

The HIGH PRIESTESS

You have intuition. An inner voice. But you may not listen to it as much as you should. Tune out the world! Calm things down and open yourself to what your deeper subconscious self is trying to say. What have you not been hearing?

Think about abundance, beauty, benevolence, and a new birth. Appreciate where you are and what you have. Ask yourself, how do you use your many gifts? What have you given to others? What have they given to you?

The EMPEROR

Consider stability, power, and authority. You can bring order to chaos, sometimes doing much by staying still. Inhabit your confidence fully and do not apologize for who you are. But even though a ruler has a throne, a ruler still serves.

The HIEROPHANT

You could be on the verge of attaining knowledge, wisdom, and blessing. You may want to go looking for advice. Seeking deeper knowledge is strongly advised. What do you have still to learn? What is it that you want to know? Who is it you can turn to?

The LOVERS

There is reason for optimism and the potential for harmony.
Things might be coming together that were long separated. You
could be on the verge of overcoming an obstacle. There are
connections to be made, and choices as well.

The CHARIOT

A significant detour may be coming. Are you going to fight your way through or just go around? Do you know your ultimate goal and how to attain it? The journey can be just as important as the destination. Except when it's somewhat tedious, more of a means to an end.

STRENGTH

There is confidence in strength. A feeling of permanence and solidity. Some may see this as victory or triumph. But it is also potentially a place of thoughtfulness and compassion for others. You have strength. But what does that mean for you?

The HERMIT

Hang back. There is no need to be everywhere at once. In withdrawal and solitude comes wisdom. Or something like it. You have a light. Use it to help yourself or possibly others. What do you see?

WHEEL of FORTUNE

Sometimes everything is a gamble. That may not be your preference, not everybody likes to leave everything hanging on a spin of the wheel. But either way, change is coming. Lean into it. Spin that wheel like you mean it.

JUSTICE

Everything has its opposite. For every up there's a down and for every injustice there is a righteous act. But the scales of the universe do not always act on their own. Have you witnessed something out of balance?

THE
HANGED MAN

Sometimes things look worse than they are. It could be time to look at everything from a newer, fresher angle. You may also be in a place of contemplation. Take the opportunity to reconsider old assumptions.

DEATH

Something is coming to an end. It might be a significant change but nothing to be afraid of. There is a chance for rebirth, renewal, and getting out of old habits. Are you ready for a new chapter of your life? Even if the answer is no, you might still want to prepare, just in case!

27

TEMPERANCE

There is a time to commit yourself fully and a time to hang back.
Sometimes we can go too far without realizing it. Maybe now is
a time to consider whether there is imbalance in your life and if
so, how you could restore it.

The DEVIL

You will want to go deep inside to get to know your subconscious self, the one some call their shadow. What do you truly want or crave? Have there been times when those desires overwhelmed you? Or did you cause inner tension by limiting yourself?

The Tower

Sudden disruption may be on the way, whether you are aware of it or not. What kind of upheavals have you had recently? How did you bounce back? Draw on that strength to face the change that is coming without fear or hesitation.

The
STAR

Hope and regeneration is always within reach. No matter what stage you are at in life's journey, you can still make a change if you want it—and if not, you can always reaffirm the greatness that is you. Have faith in yourself and your inner resilience.

The
MOON

What is the last dream you really remember? How did it make you feel? What do you think it meant? Sometimes a dream is just a dream, but other times a dream can be a signal from your imagination, suggesting new pathways to follow or warnings of what to avoid.

The SUN

There is innocence here, along with the restoration that comes after trials and tribulations. Think of renewal and strength and the source of all your joy. Imagine all that you will be able to accomplish.

JUDGEMENT

Wrongs have consequences, even if they are not always apparent at first. Have you been wronged by someone? Have you yourself wronged someone? Either case is cause for you to examine the past and determine how you will move into the future, free of burdens and judgments.

The WORLD

You are surrounded by change. But now you can contemplate permanence, stability, and the cycles of life. Maybe you are fulfilled and accomplished. Perhaps you feel there is more to be done. Is this the end of a journey or just a beginning?

THE MINOR ARCANA

At one point, the 56 Minor Arcana cards were sometimes called the Lesser Arcana. It's true that these cards do not deal with quite the same level of life-altering situations as the Major Arcana. But even though there might be some days when you might be happier to see a Six of Cups pop up rather than The Tower—bandwidth and all—that does not mean these are inconsequential cards. They deal with money, decision-making, and relationships, just to name a few topics of interest. Crucial things!

The Minor Arcana look more like the modern-day playing cards that evolved from them. They are grouped into four suits of 14 cards (10 numbered Ace to 10, and four face or court cards: Page, Knight, Queen, and King), each of which is associated with a different element, facets of life:

★ Wands: Fire, energy, creativity, spirit
   (Aries, Leo, Sagittarius).
★ Coins: Earth, money, things
   (Capricorn, Taurus, Virgo).
★ Cups: Water, emotions, intuition, feelings
   (Cancer, Pisces, Scorpio).
★ Swords: Air, intellect, knowledge,
   change (Aquarius,
   Gemini, Libra).

♡ ACE ♡
of WANDS

This is a good time to ponder the well of your inspiration. Do you have a deep and underlying passion? If so, now might be the time to follow it. Conditions may be well-suited for creation, invention, and even rebirth.

♡ TWO ♡
of WANDS

Everyone has goals. You have made some progress towards yours.
But there is still some distance to go. Making plans for the next
step of your journey can help. You may have to decide between
sticking with what you know and breaking with the past.

♡ THREE ♡
of WANDS

You are in a position of power and confidence. You have good visibility for what is to come. There is also the potential of finding a partner who can help you achieve the kind of success that you have long dreamed of.

♥ FOUR ♥
of WANDS

You have been on a journey and undergone significant change. It could be time for you to rest and recuperate. Find your place of refuge, whether with yourself or with beloved others. Consider how far you have come.

♡ FIVE ♡
of WANDS

Do not seek them out, but be aware of the conflict and dissent in your life. These struggles can be highly disruptive but can also be a source of renewal. Looks for lessons in the strife. See what you can learn.

♡ SIX ♡
of WANDS

Things are not perfect. But you have been able to marshal your skills and meet your goal. This could be a time to bask in your success.

You have already come a long way. There is no possibility that you will turn back now. But are you feeling somewhat alone in your struggle? Or are others working against you? The odds might be long though they are ultimately in your favor.

♡ EIGHT ♡
of WANDS

Things are in motion but in what direction and to what end it is more difficult to say. What do your other cards tell you? It could be time to get on the move. Take hold of that energy and use it to your advantage.

♡ NINE ♡
of WANDS

Sometimes it seems like if it isn't one thing it is another. You might feel as though your work never ends or that others are arrayed against you. But at the end of it all, you have what it takes to succeed.

♡ TEN ♡
of WANDS

You might have been taking on too much. Is there something weighing on you? A responsibility that feels more like a burden? This may be a time to think about what you have accomplished, the effort it took, and whether you should have asked for help.

♡ PAGE ♡
of WANDS

Ah, to be young and unbound by cynicism or fear. Be open to that which is new and exciting. Recall the thrill that courses through you when you are about to set off on an adventure. The tension and uncertainty, as well. It is all part of the process of renewal.

♡ KNIGHT ♡
of WANDS

You have what it takes to get things done. Let your enthusiasm and passion not only guide you but help you conquer your fears. But don't be careless! While your energy has power, make sure it takes you in the right direction.

QUEEN
of WANDS

Your confidence is an asset, as is your luck. Charm, magnetism, and optimism bring others into your orbit. Listen to your nurturing side. Be careful not to give too much.

There is a leader within you. When you point the way, others trust and follow. But what is your vision? Where are you taking them or yourself? Make a plan and be a success.

A new opportunity has presented itself. This might be your chance to achieve what you have been striving for. How do you seize the moment? Are you willing to do what needs to be done?

You have a lot going on. How are you balancing your priorities?
Are you a good enough juggler or is it time to cut back?

You have talents. But not everything you have was secured on your own. You had help along the way.

Once you have something you have long desired, it is natural to want to keep it. But try too hard and you might lose it. Protect what you have. But do not forget to enjoy it as well.

* FIVE *
of COINS

Try as you might, not everything comes up roses. When you hit a bad patch, remind yourself that help can usually be found. You just need to look around you.

Have you come into some good fortune? If so, spread the wealth!
Nothing shows your appreciation for everything you have been
given like giving to others.

SEVEN of COINS

Pausing, in work or in your journey, gives you an opportunity for rest. It can also provide a chance for reassessment. What are you laboring for, after all? Are you headed in the right direction? Maybe it is time to check that map.

You have *skills*, no doubt. But you can always be better. Consider yourself an apprentice. Be dedicated, serious, and sincere. After all, practice makes perfect.

NINE of COINS

Prosperity and achievement might be in your grasp. You have something to celebrate. Are you solitary in this state or is that independence? Learn to luxuriate.

TEN of COINS

Good things will come. Maybe they have already. Is it time to look back at what you have done, what you have gained? It could be wealth, family, or something else rare and wonderful.

★ PAGE ★
of COINS

There is much for you to learn. Contemplation is your solace.
Some might think you are dreaming, but in fact you are planning
and growing. Just be sure to watch where you are going.

KNIGHT
of COINS

All work and no play may not sound good, but it can be satisfying. You are steady, responsible. Predictable? Sometimes. But trustworthy. Do not forget: your efforts have a purpose.

* QUEEN *
of COINS

Here's a secret: Nurturing is hard work! Are you taking care of others or are you too busy taking care of yourself? Maybe things need rebalancing. Security can come at a price but it is usually worth it.

Sometimes all of your hard work can have a reward. Whether that is a material thing or something as simple but as needed as some space to relax, now could be the time to enjoy what you have.

✽ ACE ✽
of CUPS

You have five senses. They are telling you something. This is a time of emotional abundance. New relationships could be starting or older ones revitalized. You could be inspired to make a fresh start. Go with it! (But don't get carried away.)

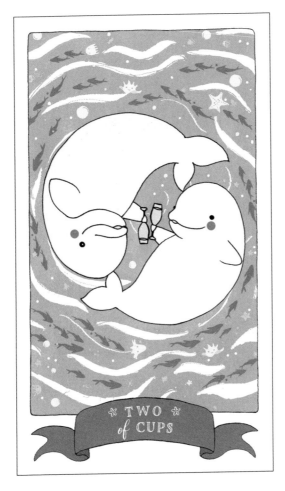

☆ TWO ☆
of **CUPS**

Two can be stronger than one. Harmony and partnership trumps
disunity. A romance could be waiting, or a new friendship. They
might be coming to you or you could have to go looking. Keep
your eyes and heart open.

You are not alone. There are people in your life to connect with—community, family, friends new and old, maybe even an old enemy who might have turned over a new leaf—or new connections to make.

FOUR of CUPS

Jumping at every chance offered you is not just bad planning, it's exhausting. But this may not last. Take advantage while you can.

You could have lost something of importance or faced a trying time with emotional consequences. But keeping your head down makes it hard to see the good that is coming.

✳ SIX ✳
of CUPS

The past is in the past, but it never disappears. Are you returning to a familiar place with strong associations? Is there a memory you cannot shake? There might be a sensation, a discovery, or even a person from earlier in your life worth revisiting.

* SEVEN *
of CUPS

Choices! So many choices. But not all are equal. Some promised opportunities can be just what you are looking for. Others can be just pretty illusions. Look closely. Take your time. Try to see clearly.

Not every victory is easily earned. There are setbacks in your journey. These can be cause for concern or a reason to recoup. Give yourself more chances. Do not be afraid to try a different path or ask for directions.

✱ NINE ✱
of CUPS

Satisfaction is its own reward. Take stock of life and love. Find pleasure in what you have achieved. Indulge yourself. Relish what life has to offer you.

TEN of CUPS

You might not have everything you want. But do you have everything you need? Think about what truly matters. It might be right in front of you, or just around the corner.

✽ PAGE ✽
of CUPS

Inspiration is like lightning, only not as dangerous (usually). It cannot be planned, it makes your hair stand up, and afterward you might look at things differently.

KNIGHT
of CUPS

New possibilities could be headed your way. Romance, adventure,
some long-desired opportunity. Be relaxed but prepared. Who
knows what form the messenger could take or whether you will
hear the message?

QUEEN of CUPS

Intuition and empathy are your guides. Sometimes you can tell what others need before they do. Other times you are searching for counsel of your own.

KING of CUPS

Maintain your balance. Rise above squabbles and negativity. Do not inhibit your feelings but direct them. Other people respect your even-handedness and wisdom. They will want your advice.

Shouting "Eureka!" may be going too far but you could have just had or be on the verge of a significant breakthrough. It may be a change in your circumstances or a new understanding of the world. In either case, savor it.

★ TWO ★
of SWORDS

There are important choices to make about your future. But the way ahead is unclear. You may feel stuck in between. However, you have all the tools you need to make your decision.

★ THREE ★
of SWORDS

Loss and pain are unavoidable. They are also not permanent. Do
not avoid what happened to you. Facing your hurt can bring it
down to size and maybe even make the next time easier to bear.

FOUR of SWORDS

While a good defense can be a good offense, sometimes an even better defense is doing nothing at all. Pulling back from the world is a perfectly fine reaction to tough times. Seek rest and recovery so that when you return you are prepared.

☆✦ FIVE ✦☆
of SWORDS

Confidence is ascendant in the aftermath of a victorious outcome.
The field is yours. But things are not always that simple. Remember
the teachings of that immortal sage Han Solo and avoid cockiness.

✫ SIX ✫
of SWORDS

Transitions might be necessary, but they can often be difficult.
The process of changing from one state of being or environment
to another may cause friction. But you can also see it as a good
time to let go of the burdens of your past.

SEVEN of SWORDS

Honesty is always the best policy. Except when it's not. There are times when stealth is the better option. But not everybody is going to agree with that. Just be ready for what may come afterwards.

EIGHT of SWORDS

Some traps we set ourselves. The good news is that those can be the easier ones to deal with once you find them. Be vigilant.

NINE of SWORDS

There is no limit to things that you can be worried about. Some can be real, but others may be just phantoms, anxieties, or figments of your imagination. Separate the real from the imagined.

Things may look dark. When dealt a serious blow, it can be easy to lose hope. But you are still standing. Now is a time for rebuilding.

PAGE of SWORDS

Focus and direction may not be your strong suit at the moment. New ideas, possibilities, dreams, and desires keep your head buzzing. You can try to harness that flow or follow it where it takes you.

KNIGHT
of SWORDS

Confident in what you believe, you charge forward with conviction.
Be certain about your course of action. Is that satisfaction from
doing the right thing or simply doing? Look before you leap.

Strength can be perceived as harshness, but it does not have to be. What you have learned and gone through has given you wisdom, as well as independence, and a strong set of principles. Use all those gifts to answer the questions you are being asked.

Being in charge can be as simple as just thinking it. Use that confidence to be decisive. Keep your standards high. Do not settle for second best. But do not forget to show compassion as well.

CONTINUE THE JOURNEY

Astrology

One aspect of reading tarot that some but not all people do is astrological. All of the Major Arcana cards have specific astrological associations, which can provide further guidance in your reading (if that's your thing).

The Fool – AIR

The Magician – MERCURY

The High Priestess – MOON

The Empress – ARIES

The Emperor – ARIES

The Hierophant – TAURUS

The Lovers – GEMINI

The Chariot – CANCER

Strength – LEO

The Hermit – VIRGO

Wheel of Fortune – JUPITER

Justice – LIBRA

The Hanged Man – WATER

Death – Scorpio

Temperance – SAGITTARIUS

The Devil – CAPRICORN

The Tower – MARS

The Star – AQUARIUS

The Moon – PISCES

The Sun – SUN

Judgement – FIRE

The World – SATURN

~ Games ~

As we mentioned earlier, the original tarot deck designs came out of card games played in Europe centuries ago. But just because the cards are today more commonly used for divination purposes doesn't mean that you can't use your tarot deck for game play.

For the classicists, you can go back to the old game play rules which developed over the years as it spread from the original Italian game of *TAROCCHI* across Europe to the variations still played in France, Switzerland, and Central Europe. Michael Dummett and John McLeod's *A HISTORY OF GAMES PLAYED WITH THE TAROT PACK* is a good guide to the background and rules of tarot game play.

For those who are less interested in learning a new game with new rules, it is not uncommon to use your tarot deck to play solitaire. Go ahead—they won't mind.

Brimming with creative inspiration, how-to projects, and useful information to enrich your everyday life, Quarto Knows is a favorite destination for those pursuing their interests and passions. Visit our site and dig deeper with our books into your area of interest: Quarto Creates, Quarto Cooks, Quarto Homes, Quarto Lives, Quarto Drives, Quarto Explores, Quarto Gifts, or Quarto Kids.

© 2022 by Quarto Publishing Group USA Inc.

Illustrations © 2022 by Hsiaochi Yang

This edition published in 2022 by Rock Point, an imprint of The Quarto Group,
142 West 36th Street, 4th Floor, New York, NY 10018, USA
T (212) 779-4972 F (212) 779-6058 www.QuartoKnows.com

Previously published as part of a kit in 2022 by Rock Point, an imprint of The Quarto Group,
142 West 36th Street, 4th Floor, New York, NY 10018, USA

All rights reserved. No part of this book may be reproduced in any form without written permission of the copyright owners. All images in this book have been reproduced with the knowledge and prior consent of the artists concerned, and no responsibility is accepted by producer, publisher, or printer for any infringement of copyright or otherwise, arising from the contents of this publication. Every effort has been made to ensure that credits accurately comply with information supplied. We apologize for any inaccuracies that may have occurred and will resolve inaccurate or missing information in a subsequent reprinting of the book.

Rock Point titles are also available at discount for retail, wholesale, promotional, and bulk purchase. For details, contact the Special Sales Manager by email at specialsales@quarto.com or by mail at The Quarto Group, Attn: Special Sales Manager, 100 Cummings Center Suite 265D, Beverly, MA 01915 USA.

10 9 8 7 6 5 4 3 2 1

ISBN: 978-1-63106-879-9

Publisher: Rage Kindelsperger
Creative Director: Laura Drew
Managing Editor: Cara Donaldson
Cover and Interior Design: Beth Middleworth
Text: Chris Barsanti
Illustrations: Lulu Mayo

Printed in Singapore